Kaleidoscope
Again, Carry On!

By Elisabeth Levy

Copyright © 2021 by Elisabeth Levy

All Rights Reserved. No part of this book may be reproduced, stored in a retrieval system, or transmitted in any form or by any means, electronic, mechanical, photocopying, recording, or otherwise without the prior written permission of Elisabeth Levy or her assigns.

Kaleidoscope: Again, Carry On! reflects the opinions, perceptions, and memories of Elisabeth Levy. The stories they express within these pages are matters of personal opinion, not necessarily fact, and are in no way intended to be hurtful to any individual or group.

ISBN: 978-1-7351438-6-6
Library of Congress Control Number: 2021920185

Section illustrations by Alexa Rhoads
Assistance to Elisabeth by Tiara Visitacion

Crafted, edited, and designed by Linda A. Hamilton
Published by Stories to Last
Oakland, CA
www.StoriestoLast.com

Stories to Last

Kaleidoscope

Again, Carry On!

By Elisabeth Levy

"Each life is a kaleidoscope of stories, reflections of color and light and patterns constantly changing, complex, wonderous, and unique."

- Anonymous

"Carry On! After my beloved husband passed away, patients and friends wrote to me about how much those two words meant to them. I have used them ever since."

- Elisabeth

Other titles by Elisabeth Levy:

2020 *Carry On: Travels Around California and the USA*
2019 *Oma Carries On: Stories from My Life*
2017 *Carry On: Travels Around the Globe*
2008 *Destiny*

TABLE OF CONTENTS

Preface	7
Introduction	9
Part I: Roots	11
Transplanted Roots & Apple Trees	12
Part II: Becoming Elisabeth	17
Sisters	18
Lemonade on a Hot Day	19
The Potato Bugs	20
Fire! Fire!	22
Christmas Time Down Memory Lane	25
My Tante Marie	30
Part II: From Nest to Flight to Nest of My Own	33
A Very Special Friend	34
Excerpts from *Destiny*	37
Learning French	44
Two Swiss Ski Adventures of a Different Kind	47
Spreading My Wings	51
The Power of Love	55
Is There a Santa	58
The Magic Suitcase	61
Part IV: Learning to Carry On	67
Celebrating Four Special Lifelong Friends	68
The Pizza Day	72
The Highest Village in Switzerland	74
My Very Last Flight	77
Epilogue	79

PREFACE

TIME

IN JANUARY OR FEBRUARY 2021, during one of our last Zoom writing classes for The Varenna Writers' Club, the assignment was to define time. How do we spend it? What does time mean for each of us personally?

Time is a very weird thing. One minute, it can feel like a hop through the grass, and two minutes later, it can feel like trying to pull a dragging donkey.

For me, time stopped in mid-March 2020. It is now almost one year since we had to be isolated, thanks to the COVID-19 virus. The dining room is closed. Food is delivered at a designated time by a masked person to our homes. At least we have Zoom classes! Some are workouts; some are lectures. But life is such as it never was in my lifetime.

With fewer functions to attend, we should have all the time in the world to do all the things we never had time to accomplish before, in our "regular" world. But what happened? It is morning, and then, it is late afternoon. The day of the week does not matter. It is the same daily routine. We get caught up in email, lunch time arrives, then nap time, and walk time. Outside the apartment, we are masked, barely recognizable. People pass each other and are afraid to stop and say hello. Yes, all of a sudden, we are all masked strangers, and so, the day passes. Time runs through our fingers without accomplishing much. Another day is gone. Usually, by the time I think I should call my friends, it is too late. Oh well, tomorrow will be another day.

I wonder, how did I spend the time before COVID-19? I hardly remember it now. I recall or think I remember that time flowed. My life was on an even keel, with thirty-one years spent in an exceedingly happy marriage. Then, slowly writing started to occupy a fair amount of my time.

Yes, time is an unpredictable thing. Can WE control it, or is IT controlling us?

INTRODUCTION

Dear Readers:

I decided to present you with another short book. This one is slightly different from those before. This is a collection of stories from the wide cloth that has made up the fabric of my life and writing. It contains stories from Switzerland, my home country, printed in previous anthologies and from the memory book, *Oma Carries On*, written just for my family. It contains more recent stories from my time at Varenna. It contains stories from my early childhood, stories from my grandchildren, old-time friends, and new-time friends. Having them all in one book is special for me. A place to remember, to share, and to paint vignettes of a long life—a sheer kaleidoscope.

***

I dedicate this book to my family, who have taken care of me since the first day of my life, and to all my friends who have touched my life through these many, many years.

Carry on as always,
Elisabeth

PART I

ROOTS

Transplanted Roots & Apple Trees

From a Zoom writing class with the subject "Roots"
February 24, 2021

WHAT IS SO SPECIAL ABOUT KNOWING our origins, our roots? I grew up in Switzerland where it would have been considered a waste of time to think about your roots. We knew where our grandparents and our great-grandparents lived, both my paternal grandparents, the Rellstabs, and my maternal grandparents, the Lutzes. I knew that our birthplace was the city of Wädenswil, where our paternal ancestors came from, a pretty place on the shores of Lake Zürich with many red-tiled rooftops. At 1,300 feet in elevation, the town rises into forested foothills with a view of the Alps to the south. It is home to prehistoric pile dwellings, which are stilt houses built over the waterways during the Neolithic Age, some 7,000 years ago. But this knowledge of where my ancestors came from was no big deal. However, this drastically changed in 1958, when I moved to the United States.

Once I came to America, I neglected my Swiss roots. Living in the USA, I quickly adjusted to a different lifestyle, and new and tender roots grew. As I began to know Americans, I realized that these people—who had come from all over the world—valued the importance of their

Elisabeth (right) with family in Switzerland

identity, their roots.

I married in America, and those roots grew happily and strong. I took good care of them. Those tender roots thrived until my very special husband died. Then part of my roots—those established in our wonderful relationship—died, too.

I thought of the few Swiss roots I still had as like a plant in a special pot. Could they be nurtured enough to regain their strength? I ventured out, traveled to Switzerland, and soon realized that—though my ancestors came from that place and I grew up there—my American roots were by far stronger and healthier. Even without my beloved, I knew with certainty that I belonged to my chosen country, where I have a wonderful family with strong roots that will last until the end of my life.

This is not the end of the story. All my life, I have

encountered situations and discoveries that keep me connected to my Swiss roots. This was one of them. When my second great-grandson, Elliott, was born February 19, 2021, my curiosity was awakened. I learned his name stemmed from the initials of his grandfather, Ernest Epley.

It was a cousin of Justin, Elliott's father and my granddaughter Rebecca's husband, who put a bug in Justin's ear about this connection. The cousin, Mark Allen Cain, had established himself in Switzerland. Ernest Epley was his and Justin's mutual grandfather and, by investigating Ernest's life, Mark discovered their family story.

Switzerland was founded on August 1, 1291. Mark traced the Epley family on the female side to the mid-1300s. The patriarch of the family, Johannes Aeppli, was the head of the prestigious Merchants Guild with headquarters in the area of Zurich. He lived in Faellanden, a small town near the city. The Aeppli families were—as their name implies—apple growers (Aeppli is an old Dutch-German spelling of apple) and had a large orchard. Today, the city still has the Aeppli sign in their crest of arms. Subsequently, the Aeppli family settled in the U.S. under the name of Epley. What a surprise and delight to discover my granddaughter's husband's veins carry pure Swiss blood! Like my own. My granddaughter was married to a Swiss. The circle was complete.

Again, Carry On!

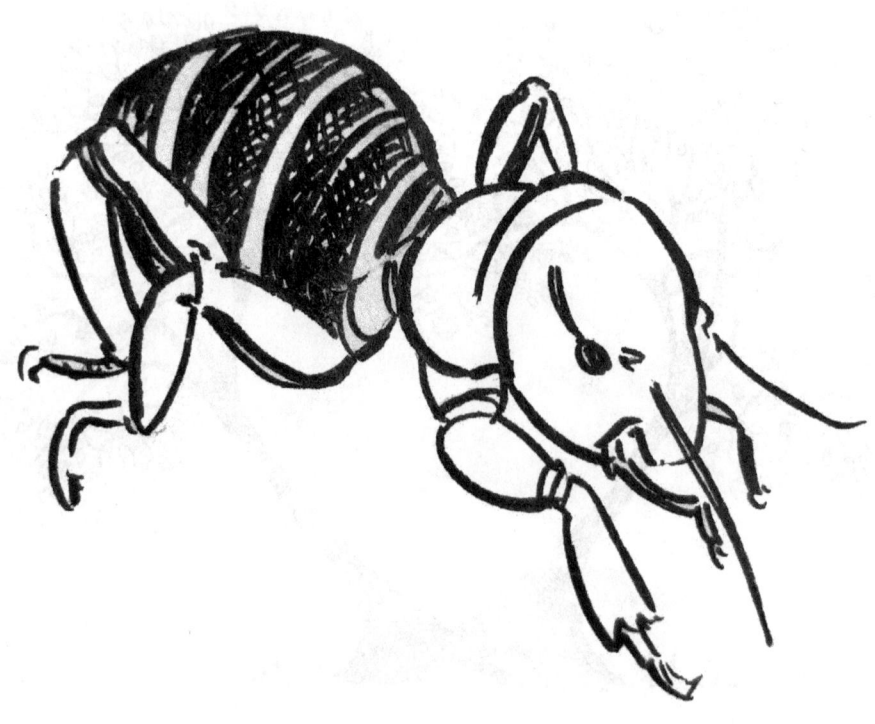

PART II

BECOMING ELISABETH

Sisters

I GREW UP WITH THREE SISTERS: Lily, ten years older; Margrit, seven years older; and Erika, six years older. My brother Heinz was eight years younger than me. Because of the age gap, I was not very close to my older sisters. However, after I was hospitalized in 2018, I started connecting with Erika. I called her every Saturday morning. We talked about our childhood memories.

Margrit died first at age ninety, Lily passed away shortly after her hundredth birthday, and I lost Erika during COVID-19. I miss her very much. Now, my brother Heinz calls me once in a while.

"The Living Stairs:" Lily, Margrit, Erika, and Elisabeth, ca. 1933

Lemonade on a Hot Day

ONE OF MY EARLIEST MEMORIES is of a Sunday outing to the Lake Lucerne area. I was about three years old. It was hot, and to my great relief and joy, my father carried me on his shoulders. We walked along the paved road beside the lake and stopped at the Hotel Seehof. I still remember the delicious, cold lemonade we drank. Kids were encouraged to run around and have fun on the grounds of the hotel. Refreshed from our drinks, we did just that. I think, this is a lasting memory because it was one of my very first excursions. It included many pleasant sensations and was exciting for a tiny child to be taken out to explore the world for the first time.

Erika, Lily, Margrit, Mother with Elisabeth on her back, and Father, taking a break from carrying Elisabeth, ca. 1930

The Potato Bugs

This story first appeared in the anthology ***Voices*** *by Oakmont Writers.*

1941

ONE EARLY SUMMER DAY, our teacher interrupted the class and announced the following message: "Listen carefully. Potato bugs have been found on the potato plants in our area, and it is up to us to avoid a potential disaster. These bugs could eat up our food. This afternoon at one o'clock, you need to be back at the front of the schoolhouse. You will be given a certain area to search. You need a pair of heavy boots, a hat, and be sure to bring a paper bag with you. The mature bugs have stripes and measure approximately ¾ of an inch. They chew the leaves, and this is what does the damage to the crops. The immature ones are more dangerous and more difficult to detect. Now, go."

Adele, the "beauty queen" of our grade, announced she would certainly wear gloves to pick up the disgusting creatures, but the boys immediately "set her straight," telling her to forget such a dumb idea. With gloves on, how would she feel any bugs?

At one o'clock, we set out with anticipation to "save the world" from the potato bugs. Volunteers, like our mothers and younger siblings, helped keep our morale up. Charley Smith, one of my classmates, always had a joke ready to make us laugh. With this team of support, we walked and searched. We looked and looked. But we found nothing. It became very discouraging, walking through row after row seemingly forever in vain.

All of a sudden, this changed. We heard our class scientist Richard yell, "Herr Ganz, what is this?"

We all ran to Richard, and sure enough there was a small, live potato bug. We found two more. Another class found some, too. The local radio station announced our success that evening on the news with pride and joy. We knew we had helped save this little enclosed Switzerland of ours from disaster.

The next day in school, we were asked to make a drawing of a potato bug. I can't draw, but I can write, and this, dear Reader, is what a potato bug looks like, if you've never seen one.

Potato bugs—also known as Jerusalem crickets—have large brown heads with a humanoid appearance. Their bodies have shiny orange and black bands. As wingless creatures, they get around on their six spider-like legs, three large legs on either side of their bodies. They can grow up to 2.5 inches (6 cm), nearly as long as the width of your hand. In fact, due to their unsightliness and size, people describe potato bugs as "the monsters of the insect world."

The idea that we as school students could be part of such an important task, to eliminate the potato bugs and save our country from starving, makes this one of my most memorable stories that I hope you have enjoyed.

Fire! Fire!

This story first appeared in the anthology
Oakmont Writers Review.

The Fire of August 3, 1941.

FIRST, THE HISTORY.
Every little and large city in Switzerland has a church, and on a designated day of every year, there is a big anniversary celebration with festivities that takes place at the church. In my hometown, the church of Kloten had been around since the eleventh century, but the existing church building was built around 1741. At the same time that the church celebrated its anniversary, the city band observed its 25th year.

People far and wide came for the festival. They camped in tents in the meadow close to the church. Food was available. Beer and wine flowed freely, and the band played happy tunes. Some people kicked off their shoes and danced barefoot.

After a day of festivities, my sister Margrit and I decided to take the ten-minute walk and go home early. Living in the Manse, the Minister's headquarters, our living rooms were on the second floor. We made ourselves comfortable in my bedroom and let our legs dangle over the windowsill, while we looked out over the neighbor's garden toward the little creek and the train station. We could still hear the band playing in the distance.

The air grew thick and heavy with an approaching storm. Gradually, the wind started to blow. Then, we saw occasional lightning strikes. We started to count the time between the lightning and the thunder. The gap between the two got shorter. Each bolt of lightning brightened the horizon, and it seemed to flash faster and faster. All of a sudden, lightning struck and thunder followed immediately in a wild and furious manner with a deafening sound. The distant music stopped abruptly. Someone shouted "Fire, fire!" Then, the church bells started to ring the warning.

Where is the fire? Margrit and I looked at each other with wide eyes. *The church? Our own home?*

We ran to the other side of the house, and, shockingly, we saw two houses across the street in flames. The firemen arrived incredibly fast but not before such great damage from the sudden lightning strike and brewing wind.

It was all commotion. Margrit and I were hit by a moment of extreme anxiety. Upset neighbors knocked on the door, wondering if their children were with us. No, they were not, we said, but we soon learned that an alert neighbor had taken them to safety right after the fire broke out.

The fire smouldered for days. The two houses we saw on fire out our window burned down to the ground. One was built in 1816. A third one was spared thanks to a fire-retardant wall. Unfortunately, fourteen cows suffered smoke inhalation and had to be killed.

In 2002, my husband and I returned to Kloten and found a small museum of local history called the Ortsmuseum Bücheler-Hus. It is located in a barn built in 1548. It was closed, but we knew how to be American charmers and succeeded in obtaining access. Among the exhibits were pictures and accounts of the fire. This visit refreshed my memory about it. I also had the opportunity to see a picture of my father next to the baptism basin in the church. Thank you, kind Kloten people for letting me reconnect with the past!

The Ortsmuseum Bücheler-Hus in Kloten

Christmas Time Down Memory Lane

This story first appeared in the anthology
Oakmont Writers Review.

DEAR READERS:
I would love to take you back to Switzerland with me, and let us all indulge in the beauty and peace of a long-past Christmas time in my hometown, Kloten, Switzerland.

Christmas season began with the four Sundays before Christmas, the Advent Sundays. On each one, our dining table was decorated with fresh pine branches, brought in from the cold, outside garden for the special Sunday evening meal.

Our supper, a piece of fresh bread and a piece of homemade cake, tasted delicious. Zopf is a special braided bread that looks similar to Jewish Challah. My mother played soft Christmas melodies on the piano, and we sang in unison "Oh Holy Night" and "Oh Little Town of Bethlehem." Frequently, we had a lonesome guest join us, a neighbor or acquaintance who lived alone.

The Christmas Angel played a big part in our celebration. We had to write a note with all our wishes and stick it on the window for the Christmas Angel to pick up while flying by. Sometimes it took a few days until the notes disappeared.

Every morning, we checked the window, waiting in

agony for the angel to visit our house on its rounds. One year, my sister Margrit behaved badly, and the next morning she found her note returned in pieces. The torn pieces were left in the space between the inside and outside glass of the window in the living room. She had to write another one.

December 6th was a famous and important day. St. Nicholas came in person to each home. At that time, he wore a gray loden coat, the type of coat everybody wore to keep the heavy rain off them. St. Nicholas had a white beard and huge gloves. We were asked to recite a poem for him or play something on the piano. The scary thing was he knew so much of our bad behavior during the year. But at the end, he told us we were basically good kids. Our hearts and shoulders relaxed. He opened his huge burlap bag and emptied the contents onto the floor—oranges, nuts, chocolate, bananas, and other edible goodies we loved. We all knew that very bad kids were put in the bag, taken to the forest, and returned the next year, so it was with great relief that we watched him close up his sack and depart.

In our huge house, we had a room we only used for Christmas. The door stayed shut until Christmas Eve, when it would be transformed for the holiday. We children looked at that closed door longingly, imagining the wonders we would see inside.

In the dining room, we had a simple dinner consisting of zopf and homemade cake. Afterwards, we sang songs in the living room until my father said he had to go downstairs to his office. We continued singing with Mother playing the piano, while we wondered if the Christmas Angel would really come. After a while, my mother asked us to be very quiet. We were anxious.

All of a sudden, we heard the clearest sound of a bell. We wanted to dash down to the lower floor, but my mother held us back. When she finally allowed us downstairs, we went slowly, fighting the urge to run. My father came out of his office.

"Did you hear the bell?" he asked.

Together as a family, we approached the Christmas Room. Light shone through the cracks of the door. When we opened the door, we saw this beautiful, big tree, decorated with candles, all of them lit with little dancing flames. An angel sat on top. We examined the tree for new ornaments, excited at each discovery, and we found our favorite ones from past years. This all happened very quickly. We couldn't wait to peek behind the thick velvet curtains. Was there anything hidden there?

Of course, there always was! One year, the surprise behind the curtain was skis. A huge gift. On a big table each of us had an assigned area with our presents. My mother had emphasized that handmade presents were worth more than bought ones. For many dark December evenings, we had worked on little handmade gifts for our parents and siblings. They were all on the table.

Before we opened the gifts, my father read the Christmas Story, how Jesus Christ was born in a manger in Bethlehem. It was hard to sit still and listen with more lovely surprises awaiting us. Our gifts always included at least one book, and the next morning, we wore coats and gloves as we read our new books in the unheated Christmas Room. We wanted to be near the tree and keep the magic of the holiday alive.

The church had their own huge tree. We, the minister's children, had to cut off the tops of the candles and loosen the wicks, and the church caretaker put them on the tree. The whole village gathered in the church on December 26th. My father took a match, lit a few candles, and soon the flames did their job, dancing upwards until all the candles were lit. We always watched in fascination. After the service, the schoolchildren received zopf.

On the last day of the year, at 11:50 p.m., members of the band walked up the stairs to the top of the church tower. They played a song to say goodbye to the old year. At 12:10 a.m., they played again, greeting the new year.

One Christmas, when I was in high school, I was in charge of a group of Boy Cubs. One of the mothers had put together some songs and poetry for us. We visited a few sick and lonesome people. We sang and recited the poetry for them and gave them each a pine branch with a shining candle and left them a few goodies. Most of the boys had never done anything like that. They were so impressed. They felt that the charitable experience was the best Christmas present they had ever received.

Again, Carry On!

My Tante Marie

This story is an excerpt from my special book **Oma Carries On: Stories from My Life**. *My granddaughter Alexa gifted me with a subscription to the website Storyworth. Every week for one year, Storyworth sent me a question about my life that I then answered. The result became my special little book for my special family.*

TANTE (AUNT) MARIE WAS MY father's older sister. I remember her only as being "old" and "waddly." At the time, she was around fifty. I never knew my grandparents, and Tante Marie was the perfect person to take their place.

Tante Marie lived in an old farmhouse in Erlenbach about twenty kilometers from our home overlooking Lake Zurich with my father's brother and family. I spent all of my summer vacation with her. It was while staying with Tante Marie that I met Simone, my paraplegic friend (whom you will read about in the next story). Tante Marie never had to get a job outside of the home. Her work was taking care of her parents, while her sister Sophie went through an apprenticeship to become a member of the working society. Unfortunately, Sophie died very young, and I never got the chance to know her. But I'm glad I got to know Tante Marie. After her parents died, Marie lived a simple but meaningful life on her small inheritance. She visited her friends, was a Sunday school teacher, and always took me with her when she went to see sick and needy people.

One time, she left me to eat with the farmers, my Aunt Elise, and Uncle Hans. For lunch, we had "waehe," a pizza-like or pie-like dish I loved, except I was used to cheese and fruit waehe only. I had no idea my Aunt Elise had made an onion waehe. I bit into a huge piece. The taste shocked me to such an extent that everybody laughed. I was made to eat the whole piece before I got a piece of apple waehe. I finished long after everybody had left the table. To this day, I always say, "No onions, please!"

The last time I saw Tante Marie, she was in a nursing home, lying in a fetal position, unable to stretch her legs. Her last words to me were "You know, I still love life."

I looked up to her because she was a very kind person and was good to everybody. She was always ready to give help to anyone who needed it.

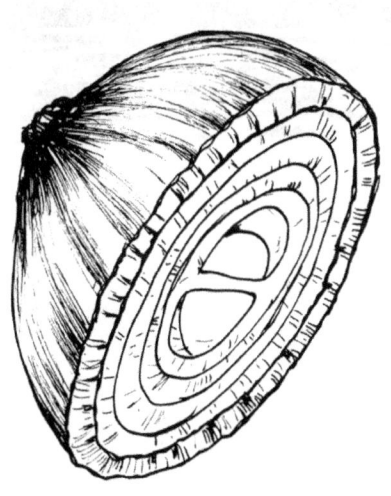

PART II

FROM NEST TO FLIGHT TO NEST OF MY OWN

A Very Special Friend

*This story appeared in its original form in **Oma Carries On: Stories from my Life**.*

SIMONE ENTERED MY LIFE at the age of ten. I was on vacation at Tante Marie's when my aunt told me a new family had arrived from France with a girl named Simone who was my age, and she wanted me to meet her. The moment I met Simone, I was smitten. Her Swiss and German were rudimentary, but I loved her accent, and her personality was charmingly French, thanks to her French mother. That year and the next summer, we had lots of fun together. We played ball games in the school playground. We went swimming together in the lake about a twenty-minute walk from Tante Marie's house. The walk was just as fun with all our chatting.

Then, the tragedy happened. In 1941, at the age of thirteen, Simone became ill with a meningitis-type disorder that paralyzed her overnight. For the next year, she stayed in the hospital. Finally, her parents were told they could take her home, but she would never walk again. After this tragedy, Simone's mother became the driving force in Simone's life. Her mother would not let Simone feel sorry for herself. This helped Simone immensely. Simone began to participate in the arts, trained and got a job as a secretary, learned to drive a car, and earned a silver medal for swimming in the Paralympic Games. I loved to visit her in the summertime.

Later on, while I was in nursing school, I was able to work with Simone at a camp for Girl Scouts with disabilities. There, she was known by her camp name, Poulain, which is old French for filly, and she was a group leader. I happily fulfilled their need for an RN. Even though she was the most severely afflicted person there, Simone inspired all of us.

Sadly, Simone's family had to endure another tragedy. On one of his mountain-climbing trips in 1944, her brother wanted to pick a few edelweiss to bring back to her. In doing so, he fell over the rocks into a crevasse and died. The family was left to grieve his untimely death. Having moved for work, I was not with Simone, but back home when I heard about the shocking news of her brother's accident.

Simone

I left for the USA in 1958. One day, I received an article written in the paraplegic newspaper of the Swiss Foundation. It was Simone's story, written by my nursing school classmate Margaret Battin.

After I lost my sweetheart in 2006, I moved to Oakmont and started to attend a writing class. It was a therapeutic as well as a welcomed distraction and activity as I grieved. I decided to translate Simone's story for my class. Another native Swiss helped me in this work. My cousin Helen Munch edited the story for me. After that, annually for a number of years, I went to Switzerland and interviewed Simone so I could gather more details of her fascinating life. A few years later, Helen and I were able to put the story together. It was the first book I ever wrote.

Simone died in April 2019. She truly was the most remarkable and wise person I had ever met, a role model for her friends and for strangers alike. Despite the tragedy that befell her, she lived a full, meaningful life, and she was always, always cheerful. She was a role model for me in many ways. She was a role model to more people than she could've imagined.

Excerpts from

Destiny: Simone, A Survivor's Story

Crafted and edited by Elisabeth Levy from interviews and Simone's handwritten notes (2008)

The Blow that Literally Blew Me Off My Feet

AT MIDNIGHT ON FEBRUARY 11, 1941, I woke up feeling extremely cold with a sharp pain like a dagger in my back. I struggled out of bed and went to my parents' bedroom, looking for warmth and comfort. Once there, I immediately fell back to sleep. At least, that's what everybody thought, but in reality I had slipped into a deep coma.

The next morning, my parents got up as usual, moving around very quietly. At seven o'clock, it was time for me to wake up and get ready for school. My mother called me, but I was pretty nonresponsive. When I finally came to my senses, I had a horrible feeling and said to my mother, "I have no legs. I can't get up." Would any mother believe such a story? Of course not, and mine didn't either.

My mother thought I just didn't want to go to school, but as soon as she started to pinch my legs and tickle the soles of my feet, with no response from me, she became very concerned. My legs had no reaction to any stimulation. In the meantime, I drifted off again and awoke some time later at the hospital. At this point, nobody imagined that this was the beginning of a life changed forever by endless problems and difficulties.

Much later, I learned that the students were let out of school in the middle of that morning, and, of course, they were very happy to learn that school would be closed for three weeks. Little did they know of the drama going on behind the scenes. Even their parents were not aware of the severity of my illness. In fact, one of our classmates had already contracted the same Encephalitis virus and had died of it. In my case, this virus led to paralysis from the seventh vertebra down…

Overnight, my life changed. From being a girl with an abundance of energy, I became a person with many physical problems and even little chance of survival. Slowly, so it seemed, everybody gave up hope, except my family. They were my "Rock of Gibraltar." We had to continue in spite of it all and not give up. My family, including my older brother, fought tirelessly against this disease called cerebrospinal meningitis.

Simone

A Life Without Legs and How to Deal With It

MY VIVID IMAGINATION was a godsend. It kept me going during my eighteen-month stay at the hospital. I dreamed of all sorts of amazing and exciting trips. I know these recollections prevented me later from drifting into depression.

Fortunately, there was a physician at the hospital who took a special interest in me. As I lay on a gurney, a sheet draped around my middle, he gently "drove" me down the hill, over cobblestone streets to Lake Zurich so I could feed the ducks and swans. After so many months of being cooped up inside a hospital, I couldn't imagine a more invigorating and exciting experience.

The physician, whose name unfortunately now escapes me, had spent a number of years in Africa, and he had lots of tales to tell. In me, he found a thankful listener. Like a sponge, I soaked up every single word. Convincingly, he told me about elephant rides in which no legs were needed to "walk" through the high grass and observe the animals. It was his way of preparing me for my life ahead. In his sensitive descriptions of a world far away, he let me imagine being carried by porters, relaxing on an ottoman, all without using my legs. I, in turn, told him about my plans; I would take big trips, paint, swim, and keep a very active life as I learned to walk again. He realized my exuberance was therapeutic, but very slowly and gently, he let the truth sink in.

I would never be able to walk again. Never.

He spent countless hours of his own free time teaching me that my paralysis was not the end of the world. I just needed to focus on different things. How well he understood me!

In spite of this upbeat influence, I found that accepting life without legs was an extremely agonizing thought for me. Especially during the night, I wondered how I could manage life as a paraplegic. Sometimes, I felt like sinking into a dark hole. Then, I would hear my mother whisper, "Continue in spite of everything."

How to Deal With Me at Home

I FINALLY CAME HOME. It is difficult to imagine what it was like to care for a parapletgic without all the gadgets we have today. We learned to improvise. My mother was a master at it. For one thing, we had to heal my large bedsores. Dr. Karl Schonenberger, our neighbor's friend, who had just returned from India, brought back some pure eucalyptus oil. It was very expensive, but it lessened the stench of the wound, and slowly, the bed sores healed. Until that process was complete, I had to lie on my stomach.

My mother taught me another lesson: "You cannot only receive. You have to give too." I learned how to paint and to make cards, which I gave to every visitor to take home. This lesson was very valuable, preventing me from becoming a cantankerous, self-absorbed person. Staying in contact with my neighbor via the Morse code system engaged my brain, and my books kept me stimulated. My other motto: Read, Read, READ!

Girl Scouts in Spite of It All

"Pfadi Trotz Allem"

AT THE AGE OF FIFTEEN, my bed sores healed. I advanced to the next stage, using a wheelchair; in fact two wheelchairs, one for the apartment and one for street use. I had to manipulate them with my own strength as they had no mechanical parts. At first, my mother helped me to hang my legs over the bed. Then, with the aid of a rope, I learned to pull myself up. Finally, the glorious day arrived when I was able to sit in the wheelchair!

I was fortunate to meet other Girl Scouts with disabilities. Their motto: "Pfadi trotz allem"—Scouts in spite of it all. We had so much in common, and it was right in sync with my own motto: "Continue in spite of it all." It helped me enormously to be among teens and young women with the same or similar handicaps,

Simone and the Girl Scouts having fun *in spite of it all*

and it taught me that caring for each other makes everyone's life easier. Never mind the wheelchairs, they were just an added necessity...

This group of handicapped Girl Scouts also showed me that in spite of my disability, I could lead a relatively normal and independent life. They inspired me, instilled courage in me, and after a few short months, they chose me as their leader—We were very creative—learning to cook sumptuous meals while lying on our tummies. For us, the word "impossible" did not exist.

Simone's silver metal for backstroke in the 1960 Paralympic Games in Rome

Simone doing her graphic arts

Simone and Elisabeth

Learning French

I GREW UP IN THE GERMAN PART of Switzerland, where our second language was French. While I was in eighth grade, I traveled to the French part of Switzerland as an exchange student. Fortunately, in my new household, there was a girl who was only a few years older than me. Marie-Louise and I immediately bonded. We bicycled through the sparsely populated countryside with vineyards galore interspersed with castles. The beauty is indescribable, the trailing green leaves of the vines and the red of the grapes in rows on the hillsides, and flowers on the borders on either side of country lanes that led to stately gray stone castles, like wizened old men among the budding fruit.

The house was an old farmhouse without running water. Madame Marendaz left me a pot of water in my bedroom for washing up. Well, she did not know me yet.

My bedroom was on the ground floor facing a lovely courtyard with a fountain. I easily climbed outside to use the fountain for my morning toiletry. It was no big deal for me.

Little did I know that Madame M. had just lost her husband. I was a happy-go-lucky teen, and having a young, enthusiastic girl in the house seemed to help her in her grief. She started to call me her "sunshine." Yes, I had a wonderful time learning French with these two ladies, Madame M. and Marie-Louise. However, on Mondays, I had lessons with a French woman with a wrinkly old face. I am sure I did not say the nicest things to express my displeasure about this Monday class.

Later, after high school, I had a year to fill before going to nursing school. I decided to improve my French and took a job in the French part of Switzerland. I took care of a five-year-old girl, Luce, while her mother, Madame Landolt taught school. They lived in a hamlet called Cheseaux-Noreaz located at least five miles from the closest city, Yverdon. This place DID have running water. But it was still simple country living. The family's apartment was above the school room. When I was in my bedroom, I could stretch out my arms and touch both sides of the room.

Luce was a spoiled brat, and the previous governess was not able to handle her, so I had my hands full. But Luce came around. The downstairs school had about twenty students from first to sixth grade. On the very first day, I noticed during the break that the students stood outside the classroom like zombies. I took Luce with me, and in short order, we began to play games with them, various ball games and climbing the ropes. We invented games.

Luce was a good sport. There were other schools like ours, and once in a while, we were able to get together and play in competition, basketball, volleyball, and track and field games. Luce and I had fun firing our team up with cheers and yells. We loved seeing them do well. Luce became sociable under my care.

I accompanied Luce and her mother on a summer vacation in the "big" city of Yverdon-Les-Bain, a population of 7,000 at the time. Yverdon is located on Lake Neuchatel. Luce learned to swim that summer.

Sadly, many years later, Madame Landolt and Luce were killed in Yverdon by a drunk driver. They had taught me better French. And a lot more. I miss them.

Two Swiss Ski Adventures of a Different Kind

A Ski Trip With Strings Attached

WHEN THE YOUNG MAN in my ski club offered to take me skiing, I had no idea the silliness that awaited me.

I was thirty-one years old, working and living in Zurich, Switzerland. It was shortly before I moved to the United States. Though I was a mediocre skier at best, I joined a ski club. I liked skiing. It was fun to go down the hill, make your turns and see how the run finished out. But I belonged to the club mainly to meet people, particularly men. At the time, I felt I needed a new boyfriend.

So, sure enough, when Hans, a fellow member of the ski club, came along and invited me to go skiing with him, I said, "Sure, why not."

He told me he would pick me up very early the next morning.

At 6 a.m. I waited with my skis at the place where the ski club usually met up to drive to the slopes. This beaten and banged up little car puttered up in front of me, skis attached on the passenger side of the car with strings. I looked at it in shock. How would it ever make it up into the mountains? The car was so small and ill-equipped for winter travel. It was impossible!

I watched as Hans undid his skis from the strings and tied mine on, adding his on top. He ran the strings inside the passenger side window, secured the ends inside and rolled the window shut. It looked crazy. Then, he ushered me inside the impossible little car, and I thought, "Oh my God!"

The car moved at a snail's pace out of Zurich and up the mountain roads. We left shortly after six and arrived at Andermatt—an hour and a half drive in summer—at two o'clock in the afternoon.

We had lunch at the resort and skied for no more than an hour before the slopes closed. He strung our skis back on the car and dropped me off at home in Zurich at 10:00 p.m.

That was the end of that friendship! I personally was so disgusted, I didn't want to see him again. It turned out his personality matched the car, just as impossible.

When I think back today, I cannot believe that I went skiing with such a silly person.

Sayonara and good-bye!

A Kindergarten Ski Trip

THAT SAME YEAR, my friends, Susanna and Margaret, and I decided to go skiing together. Susanna's father was the dermatologist I worked for, and we all lived in Zurich. But, this was a special occasion, because the three of us didn't ski together normally. Margaret was an expert skier, Susanna was mediocre, and I was the weakest member of the group. So, we decided it would be a "kindergarten" trip, skiing on easy slopes, or what we thought would be easy.

We left Zurich around 8:00 a.m. and arrived at the foot of Saentis (or Säntis) Mountain, the highest peak in the Alps of northeastern Switzerland, at about 11:00 a.m.

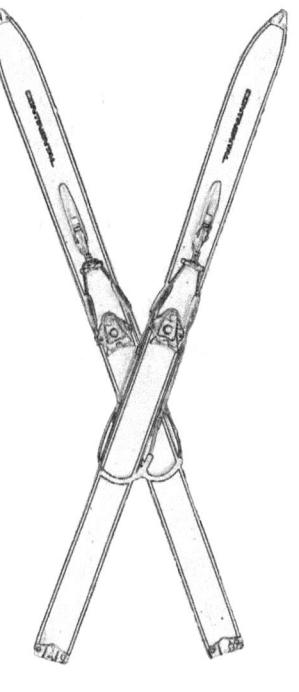

Given our time of arrival, we decided to have lunch first. When we finally hit the slopes, the snow was already very slushy.

Margaret and Susanna suggested, since I was the slowest of the three of us, that I should go first. Down I went, making one turn and and then the next, then the next, but NOT the one after that!

I was headed straight for the trees where I fell into a hole next to a tree, bottom first, my skis still on. I just sat there for a long time, scared. I didn't want to move. I was tempted to stay there. But of course, my two friends would be waiting for me, worried. Eventually, I calmed myself down enough to crawl out on my own and continue down the hill, thrilled when I finished the run in one piece.

Next down the hill came Susanna. She only fell down once in the slushy snow, immediately got up again, and skied down to join me. While Susana and I recovered, Margaret elegantly skied down and joined us. At first we didn't say a thing. Then, we all looked at one another and said, "This deserves a good meal."

We had a super dinner together at the resort, and over that delicious meal, we chatted and laughed about our "kindergarten" ski trip.

Why call it a "kindergarten" ski trip, you might ask. To me, "kindergarten" is always connected with innocent children of four or five years olds having no worries, being able to play and be themselves. It gives me a good feeling to know that innocent, small children can just BE children. And that's how I felt with Susanna and Margaret that day!

Spreading My Wings

AROUND 1956, I FELT A CHANGE was in order. I had worked for five years as a nurse in a dermatologist's office in Zurich and was happy. However, I felt it was time to spread my wings. I was in my early thirties, and it was time to see the world. I had an offer to take care of a small child in Hong Kong. That sounded very interesting to me, but my sister Erika had just left for the USA, and my mother rightly felt it would make more sense if we both went to live in the same country. I agreed and prepared to get a visa.

I was awaiting my visa about six months later, when one morning, the office doorbell rang. Much to my surprise, my classmate from nursing school, Margaret Gabathuler stood at the office door. I let her in and we made a date for lunch. While visiting friends, she had heard of my "wanderlust." She had already spent a number of years in San Francisco and had returned for some vacation time in Switzerland. She was scheduled to go back to the USA on a freighter. She suggested I travel with her so we could be together.

A freighter was not my first choice of travel, but both Margaret and I were on a budget. We had settled on the slowest and cheapest passenger ship from the Holland America Line, the Maasdam. It would take ten days to sail from Dover, England to New York.

It took a year for my visa to come, then things moved quickly. I packed while Margaret took care of getting the tickets through her travel agent.

In 1958, I said goodbye to Switzerland, the only place

I had known up until then, and boarded a train to Belgium to take in the World Exhibition, which took place outside of Brussels. Exhibits included the Atomium, a giant model of a unit cell of an iron crystal, a facsimile of Sputnik, and pavilions from many countries, but I was too excited about going to America to take much interest.

From there, I took another train and ferried across the English Channel to Dover, England.

In the meantime, Margaret had taken the train directly to Dover to board the ship. On the train, she happened to sit across a fellow who introduced himself as Tommy Wiskemann. He noticed that his suitcase had the same destination label as hers. It was a delightful coincidence, and Margaret introduced me to Tommy on the dock.

Boarding the ship, we made ourselves comfortable in our stateroom and went on deck where we met a few other young people. Tommy joined us later.

We truly had the best time during the ten-day voyage. Every night, we went dancing with the young people we met. During the day, we walked around the boat and enjoyed the sun. We laughed a lot about everything, like how they served the same potato dish every night in the dining room but each time under a different name. For several meals, an older gentleman joined us at our table. He ordered champagne for himself and me. But the other guys in our group made sure he was never able to have a dance with me. I was glad. I wasn't interested in him in the least. He was too old and didn't fit in the group.

When we arrived in New York, my sister Erika was waiting for me at the pier. She had driven her Ford—which used more oil than gasoline—from Miami to New York to meet me. Our cousin, Hellmuth, who lived in the vicinity of New York, was also in the welcoming committee. It had been so long since I had seen Hellmuth that it was like meeting him for the first time. I said goodbye for the time being to Margaret, Tommy, and the rest of our group. We made plans to meet up later, since we were all staying at the same hotel.

Hellmuth took Erika and me to his social club for lunch. He introduced us to people, and I shook their hands. My face turned purple-red when Hellmuth explained that shaking hands was not a custom here.

At the hotel, Erika and I met up with my shipmates Margaret, Tommy, and another young woman named Agnes. We all piled into Erika's car and started our adventure to the West Coast.

In Chicago, Tommy made a wrong turn and we got pulled over. He showed his complicated Swiss driver's permit to the policeman who took one look at it, shook his head, and let us go. Going west, we stopped at every landmark there was. So many that it eventually became boring to me.

Agnes had relatives in Wisconsin. At a roadstop, she went off to a phone booth to call them to let them know she would be arriving soon with friends. When she returned to us, she said with a sad expression, "They don't want to see you."

None of us could understand this, wondering what the issue might be. We took Agnes to their house to drop her off, but when we arrived, her relatives welcomed all of us inside. They had prepared a generous dinner for all five of us and invited us to spend the night. What had happened?

We realized something was lost in translation. Language problems can definitely play a big part in misunderstanding each other!

From Wisconsin, we continued driving West until it was time for our group to split up and take different highways. It might have been in Utah. Margaret and Tommy left for San Francisco, while Erika and I ended up in Portland, Oregon. I liked Portland very much. We both stayed in Portland for a while, working in Saint Vincent's Hospital.

I planned to stay maybe a year or two and then return to Switzerland. Now, after sixty-plus years, I am still here in America. The spur-of-the-moment decision I made in 1956 paved the way for what the rest of my life and what I was destined to do–become an American citizen, establish my career, and find my incredible and truly special husband.

The Power of Love

This story first appeared in the anthology
Kaleidoscope by Oakmont Writers.

***

About the Oakmont Anthologies:
Moving to Oakmont after my husband died meant a different life had started for me. I was fortunate to find a writer's group under the guidance of Kathy Rueve. We had to read our writings, and I was always surprised how the class loved my stories.

***

I WAS ASKED AN INTRIGUING question: "What or who influenced your decisions in your life, and what was the driving force?"

I couldn't write a response immediately. I did not know. Then, I realized it was definitely my granddaughter, Rebecca Jennifer Levy. I did not have any children on my own, and becoming a grandmother was a dream come true.

This baby was the daughter of my husband's son David and his wife Rita. Early in their married life, they had left for Hawaii for a short trip. When they returned to live near us, we were thrilled. It wasn't long after they had settled in that they presented my husband and I with a gift, a license plate that read, "Happiness is being a grandparent."

My heart jumped and soared. I was going to be a grandmother! My husband Bill and I would be Opa and Oma. I sheepishly asked the mother-to-be if I could take care of the baby one day a week, and Rita happily agreed.

For Christmas 1983, the children gave us a crib with all the necessary items for when the baby came to visit us. On June 4, 1984, Rebecca Jennifer Levy was born.

That very evening, the new Opa and Oma drove excitedly to the hospital to greet their twelve-hour-old granddaughter, Rebecca. I sat her on my lap, looked at her, and said, "Good evening, Rebecca Jennifer Levy, this is your Oma talking to you."

She heard my words, opened her beautiful big eyes for the first time, and looked at us. What a moment that was! The happy father also saw his daughter's beautiful eyes for the first time. As for Rebecca and me, our bond was sealed.

When her early nursing period was over, Rita brought Rebecca to our house every Wednesday. She responded so well to whatever I had planned for her to do. I put a crayon on the table, and she immediately grasped it. Without another word, she started to make a drawing. I sometimes took her swimming or walking around the hill. We checked out the flowers in the garden and sat on the steps while I read to her. In the afternoon, she would get her bath in the kitchen sink.

Early in the morning, Rebecca and I started preparations for that evening's dinner. After our day of activities, we were ready to welcome the working family members over for the evening meal. After having enjoyed the company and the food, the young Levy family would leave for home while Bill and I discussed the events of the day.

When school started, Rebecca declared she was not able to attend school on Wednesdays. That was her "Oma Day!" It was difficult, but eventually, she got used to the new schedule and came to our house after school. To our chagrin, in 1994, the family moved to New York. David was needed in his father-in-law's business. The Oma Days came to an end.

We always celebrated Christmas Eve at our house. We started this tradition after we got married and continued it until Christmas 2019.

In April 2020, time stood still. Because of Covid, the family was unable to spend Christmas together. But Rebecca and I are still close. She Facetimes me every Sunday. I see her and her family when we can get together, including my great-grandchildren Liam, running around the house, and Elliot, Liam's younger brother, in his crib.

Is There a Santa?

This story first appeared in the anthology **Kaleidoscope by Oakmont Writers.**

MOVING TO OAKMONT, after my husband died, meant a different life had started for me. I was fortunate to find a writer's group under the guidance of Kathy Rueve. We had to read our writings, and I was always surprised how the class loved my stories.

Christmas with the family was always fun, but I remember one Christmas as our most delightful. At the same time, we also experienced a very stressful event on this particular holiday.

It was the first Christmas after the young Levy family had moved from San Rafael to New York. We prepared our house to make everybody comfortable. David and Rita would use the study, and Ann and Jeff, my stepdaughter and her husband, would sleep in the guest bedroom. We thought it would be fun for the kids, Rebecca, Matthew, David William, and Alexa, to sleep in the living room. Towards the evening, we all decided to take a walk around our hill. There was a house being built in the neighborhood, and some workers teased Matthew. With a grin, they wondered aloud if Santa would visit him. Had he been good that year? They asked him.

"I am Jewish. I don't believe in Santa," Matthew answered. I think it was a good answer.

That evening, the children got ready for bed. The stockings hung neatly over the fireplace. David W. and

Matthew discussed the matter of Santa and decided, just to be on the safe side, to leave some milk and a cookie for Santa. They could watch and see what happened as they would be up all night anyway. Of course, the kids fell fast asleep. Before the adults went to bed, they removed the empty stockings, filled them, and tiptoed back into the living room to leave them in place.

The morning dawned. All of a sudden, Bill and I, asleep in our bedroom next to the living room, heard whispers and pretty soon the door opened. Our four excited grandchildren entered, one behind the other, each with a stocking full of goodies. They made themselves comfortable on our bed and checked out their presents. All of a sudden, Mathew said, "I have to tell my father that Santa really came. He ate the cookies and drank the milk."

Later that day, we decided to go for a hike around Lake Phoenix in Marin County. We planned to take the young Levy family to Switzerland in the summer and use this outing around Lake Phoenix as a training session. We started walking, and all of a sudden, David said, "Where is Matthew?"

We split up and walked around the lake, calling his name. No Matthew. We began to worry. We had heard daily news accounts about children being kidnapped and killed. We asked others on the trail. No one had seen a little boy in a red T-shirt. We went down to the parking lot. There was no sign of him there. We yelled. No response. In total agony, we returned to where the trail started. What had happened to Matthew? Where was he? We felt an anguish beyond words. All of a sudden, to our thankful relief, there was Matthew coming up the stairs. There were hugs and tears.

Later, much later, we were able to put the story together. Matthew had run ahead and taken the wrong path. When he realized it, he went back to the parking lot. He saw a lady he felt he could trust. Only later did we find her note on the windshield of our car. She took him in her car to the ranger station and brought him back to the parking lot where we finally reconnected.

I believe, none of us had ever experienced such despair either before or since that event.

Again, Carry On!

The Magic Suitcase

This story first appeared in the anthology
Kaleidoscope by Oakmont Writers.

IN 1986, ANN AND JEFF moved from San Rafael to Valencia in Southern California. Their first home was in an incredibly beautiful orange grove. Right in front of their home were bushy green-leafed trees with round, juicy oranges waiting to be picked by anybody who wanted them.

Later, they moved to another house in Valencia closer to town for convenience. While we were in Switzerland, their son David William was born on June 11, 1987. Jeff and Ann had a hard time tracking us down to tell us the news. We received the news in Switzerland, the night before we were to travel to Italy. I remember most clearly that first day in Italy purchasing a little sailor's suit for our new grandson at a big marketplace. I was thrilled and couldn't wait to see the baby. When we finally did, Ann dressed baby David in the new outfit. It was cute, and we were happy we bought it.

Because we worked and had a very busy practice, there were only infrequent visits between Marin and Southern California. Three weeks later, they shared some wonderful news. Ann and Jeff had brought baby David William to our home. It was a warm day, and the baby was wearing a bonnet. Oma immediately took him into her arms. We were very happy every time they came and visited us. By this time, David William was eighteen months old. That's when they announced: Ann was pregnant again.

It was a very special day on September 12, 1989. My

husband Bill—known to most as Dr. Levy—and I went to the office as usual. Shortly before noon, Jeff called and said he had just taken Ann to the hospital. She was in labor and they were waiting for their second baby to be born. One and a half hours later, Jeff called us again. Alexa Miriam Rhoads had safely arrived. I made plane reservations to leave the next day. Bill would join us for the weekend, having to stay to see patients during the week.

Once I was there, I immediately became involved in the care of both my granddaughter Alexa and her mother Ann. After the birth, Ann had become very sick. She was diagnosed with Giardia. a parasitic contamination of food. After Ann was discharged from the hospital, Jeff and I helped care for Baby Alexa.

At their home, I took care of Alexa and Jeff took care of David William. To take care of the newborn baby was a special privilege. I sang to her and talked to her, changed her diapers, and prepared her bottle and fed her. Jeff was worried but had to stay strong for the family. What a relief when Opa arrived! We were all so relieved when Ann felt better, recovered from the Giardia but tired.

When the family moved to Las Vegas in 1993, we visited them there once a year. At times I had to ask myself, are we really in Las Vegas? The neighborhood was very quiet, nothing like the neon, bustling strip of casinos the city is known for. But then, there would be small reminders. Yes, we were in Vegas. There were truly slot machines in stores and restaurants.

Bill and I always brought the same suitcase with us. The grandchildren began to see that suitcase as something magical. As soon as we arrived, settled in, and sat down to chat with our daughter, David W. and Alexa would look through the suitcase. To their disappointment, they didn't find a single toy.

However, the next morning, the grandchildren would wake up their sleeping grandparents and get permission to check the suitcase again. To their happy surprise, David and Alexa always found a few toys during this second search. Thus, the children coined the phrase, "The Magic Suitcase," and they went through this same routine for years.

One year, the unimaginable happened. Oma left the toys at home. How embarrassing and unbelievable! Fortunately, Oma knew she could rely on the special and kind Opa. First, of course, he had to comfort her.

The next morning, Opa and Oma pretended to be asleep when David and Alexa happily came in to wake them up. By then, they were teenagers. Soon, Opa had one of the grandchildren under each arm and started to talk to them. He began by telling them that they were now young adults. The magic suitcase had done its work and would now be closed. Would they have any idea why and what would happen next? No, they did not. Opa patiently explained that the magic happens for little children who believe in Santa, in the Christmas angels, and all the mysteries of the holiday. The children were old enough by then to know the reality of where the gifts came from. "The magic suitcase will have to wait until your own children are ready to open it." David and Alexa understood the message, pondered over it, and that was the end of the magic suitcase.

There were other memorable events that happened while the Rhoads family still lived in Las Vegas. It was easy for me to catch a direct flight from San Francisco and arrive in Las Vegas in no time. Fortunately, we had excellent employees and whenever the Rhoads needed help, my wonderful husband let me immediately fly out to Las Vegas, and it did not affect his office too much.

One morning, Ann called. She was crying on the phone. David had received an F in fourth grade math and had to be disciplined. Ann and I studied psychology books on how to approach this problem and help David figure out what his problem was, and I immediately flew out to Vegas. I am sure it impressed him that this was so serious, since Oma needed to arrive all the way from her home in Marin. After Ann and I talked to him, he worked hard and passed the subject.

David found his way. He soon became an Eagle Scout like his Opa and his father, and he diligently worked on a project, putting sand and dirt on a very slippery and dangerous corner of the bike path close to their home. His work earned David a special place in the history of the Eagle Boy Scouts. To this day, the plaque honoring David Rhoads still exists. Yes, David, we are very proud of you.

Having all these memories is really special to me. I do hope, dear readers, reading about them, you think so, too.

PART IV
LEARNING TO CARRY ON

Celebrating Four Special Lifelong Friends

Here are four examples of friendship, of lifelong ones and others met along the way, and the things we do for each other.

MY CHILDHOOD FRIEND since kindergarten, Gretli Moos Zumwalt, lives in San Diego, and to this day we call each other on our birthdays, Gretli's in June and mine in August. We used to always speak strictly Swiss German to each other, even though we both lived in California. We did this to practice our native tongue. After Gretli's husband passed away on March 18, 2013, she didn't have anyone with whom she could practice pure Swiss German anymore, except me. And I couldn't practice German with my sister Erika. I wanted to, but every time we talked, our words became a mix of German and English, like a stew. Gretli and I speak mostly in English now. Our friendship has never wavered and is essentially the same as it was in kindergarten.

***

I REMEMBER WHEN EVA'S DAUGHTER Claudia was born in a hospital in Zurich. It was a sunny June day. I took care of Eva's husband Peter and son Werner while Eva recovered from childbirth in the hospital and nursed her new baby. She was there for about a week. During that time, I did most of the grocery shopping for the family and, at their home, cooked some of their meals. Her husband

Peter also cooked some.

Werner was about four years old. In the evenings, he and I took to sitting on the rooftop deck above their detached garage eating cherries. Being June, they were ripe and juicy. We had a contest to see who could spit them the farthest distance. Werner thought that was great.

I distinctly remember their family dog. It was a Saint Bernard, a huge animal with a deep bark that was very protective of us. Evidently, if someone nearby was being hurt by someone else, the dog would bark at the attacker and try to help the victim. It was instinctive.

It was a good week with Eva's family. I felt happy supporting a friend in her time of need.

***

I HAD A MOST INTERESTING ENCOUNTER while I was in nursing school. I met up with my friend Helen at Bellevue Square (Bellevueplatz) in Zurich, beside the lake, one of the central meeting points for roads and public transportation in the city, including a huge tram station. We were standing on the platform waiting for our train when a girl our age passed by and greeted Helen. The girl was introduced to me as Ruth Braendli. The name did not mean much to me. However, my name, which was Heidy Rellstab at the time, intrigued Ruth.

"Are you by chance the minister's daughter from Kloten?" she asked.

When I replied, "Yes." She smiled.

"That means we are relatives. Our parents are cousins."

Our families had not been in much contact. Yet, we both remembered that on every New Year's Eve, my father would call her family to wish them a Happy New Year. Ruth and I became friends from that time on.

After my husband died and I had to travel alone, I would always spend my time in Switzerland with Ruth after visiting my sister Erika. I stayed in Ruth's house, where I had my own room. We did many fun things together during our visits. She and I enjoyed dinner out or cooked in. We visited Juf, the highest village in Switzerland, with her brother. We went swimming together. These are times I still treasure, looking back.

For me, it is important to keep and renew friendships.

***

YOU NEVER KNOW HOW A NEW FRIEND will come into your life. My friend Sylvia came into mine unexpectedly. I had been living in San Francisco for about six months, working as a nurse. When I needed to find living quarters, I toured several furnished apartments. One of them felt very "Swissy," adorned with Swiss-styled furnishings. It felt very pleasant. The lady renting it was indeed Swiss. She was ready to return to Switzerland and not quite ready to sell the place. I agreed to rent the apartment from her. She asked me to keep an eye on a friend of hers named Sylvia who would be arriving in the U.S. shortly. She wanted me to help Sylvia adjust to the new culture. So, I did just that. Sylvia was charming, and we bonded very quickly, even though she was much younger than me. I helped her as she found her footing, renting an apartment in Oakland.

One evening, she called me. "Elisabeth, I bought an artichoke. I cooked it for twenty minutes, and it is still stone hard." In different countries, we have different vegetables. Artichokes don't grow in Switzerland. I laughed hearing her story. I gave her instructions on how to cook it, and she was successful in doing so. We were getting to know more about each other, and I had the feeling we would become good friends.

After a few months, Kurt Meier, Sylvia's fiance—also from Switzerland—arrived in San Francisco. He was a super charmer. Everybody liked him. I helped Sylvia with wedding preparations and, before too long, we happily celebrated Sylvia and Kurt's wedding in Sausalito, California. My husband Bill was the best man.

When their first daughter Sybille was born, they asked me to be her godmother. I was thrilled and honored to be chosen.

Sylvia and Kurt died tragically while Sybille and her sister Corinne were very young. Sylvia took her own life when she found out Kurt was unfaithful. Kurt, not long after, died of a heart attack right in front of his two daughters. It was all terribly difficult for the two girls. But Sylvia's parents in Switzerland took the girls under their care. To this day, I am still in touch with my lovely godchild, Sybille, her wonderful husband Georg and their delightful children, Jan, Julia (now in medical school), and Benjamin. COVID-19 spoiled Jan's and Julia's plans for travel, but they are doing their best in their home country.

A few good friends are very important. They give you love and support, unconditionally. It's hard to feel completely alone when your heart is full.

The Pizza Day

This story first appeared in the anthology
Kaleidoscope by Oakmont Writers.

AS USUAL, I WAS SPENDING my "Swiss time" staying with my cousin Ruth in Zollikon, overlooking Lake Zurich. I made this pilgrimage every year after Bill died until Ruth also passed away. One day, her nephew Hannes and his wife Barbara invited us and friends to join them in Samstagern to make pizza.

It was a gorgeous late summer day when Ruth and I left her house and took the car ferry across the lake from Meilen to Horgen. We drove on narrow roads through the most idyllic area, with the trees just changing colors. We passed an orchard. Ripe apples hung on the branches. We stopped by and said hello. A family was selling this fruit right in front of their house. We didn't buy any because we had our own, but it was a fun break in the trip.

Finally, we turned off the main road onto an even smaller road that ran along a little lake. Way up at the end of the road, we saw the Braendlis' house, a converted barn and quite lovely. We were warmly greeted and ushered inside. The family had made the barn into a very comfortable living area. It also was Barbara's workplace where she made special bread that she sold in Waedenswil at her own small store. They were huge loaves, weighing about three pounds each, made from her own recipe. However, for the party that evening, her husband made the pizza dough.

Quite a few guests had already arrived when we got

there. Right in front of their house, they had set up a long table that could seat approximately thirty people on either side. They showed us to our seats among the others and offered us appetizers like mild sausages and corn chips with ajvar dipping sauce, made out of paprikas. We nibbled happily on these treats. As we did so, we introduced ourselves (me, the American!) and eventually, the real fun started.

On another big table we found all different kinds of pizza ingredients—cheese, tomatoes, Italian sausages, pesto sauce, pickles, and more. We learned that when making a pizza, it was important to stretch the dough to the absolute right size with a rolling pin. One of the guests gave us instructions. I rolled my own dough. Ruth rolled hers. Then, we put on our selected ingredients and took them into the kitchen to place in one of their four industrial-sized ovens to bake. Before too long, we retrieved them and returned to our seats.

It is such a delight to eat your own hand-made pizza. Ruth and I sat next to each other comparing ours. It was also fun to sample the pizza our friends had made. Of course, we thought ours tasted the best!

Linden tea was served throughout the meal. This delicious drink is made by brewing the dried flowers and sometimes the leaves and bark of the Linden tree. It not only tastes great and has a wonderful aroma, but also has been used for medicinal purposes for hundreds of years.

A homemade, delicate chocolate mousse topped off this fun and special adventure.

The drive home was equally unbelievable, beautiful with all the fall colors fading into the reds of sunset into a dusk blue-gray sky, all the light disappearing into a dark, sparkling night.

The Highest Village in Switzerland

This story first appeared in the anthology
Oakmont Writers Review.

*Juf/Avers, Viamala Region, Grisons Canton
Elevation approx. 7,000 feet (2,126 meters); Population 145*

THE YEAR WAS 2007, and I went again to Switzerland to stay with my cousin Ruth Braendli in her house with a view of Lake Zurich and the hills of the Albis. When the sky is clear, you can see the snowcapped mountains of the Alps in the far distance.

It was my second trip after my husband had died. I was traveling to forget the sorrow of losing him, and I looked forward to the trip and seeing Ruth. It was exciting.

Ruth has a brother named Werner who lives with his wife Christine in Zillis, a mountain village in the canton of Grison. They invited us to visit them for the day at their home in Zillis. We decided to travel by train.

The train ride starting in Zurich was spectacular. At first, the mountains were far away. Then all of a sudden, as we passed by, they soared into the sky right above us and just about touched the water of the Walensee, also known as Lake Walen, one of the largest lakes in Switzerland. In Chur, we transferred to the colorful yellow PostAuto, the regional bus service, and a curve-rich road took us along the Rhein River to Zillis in the Viamala Valley.

Juf/Avers

Werner and Christine—who was born in this area—did not want us to waste any time.

"Hop in the car, we'll take you to Avers/Juf," Werner said, nearly the moment we arrived.

Did I hear correctly? Avers/Juf is the highest village in all of Switzerland, at an elevation of about 7,000 feet, way above any forest. Only Arven, a type of pine, grows at that altitude and is used for building houses. With the shortage of wood, the villagers used cow dung to produce heat in their homes.

We took different modes of transportation to get to the top. Once we arrived, we stood in the middle of the village nestled into a hillside, and drank the water right from the faucet of the public well. No ice cubes were needed! The water came right from the mountains, fresh and cold. Around us, the rugged and massive rocks of the towering mountains were so close. You felt you could almost reach out and touch them. The place was absolutely gorgeous.

Next, we visited the schoolhouse. Starting in September, Christine was going to be teaching at this brand-new, modern schoolhouse. There were about sixteen students including children from the surrounding areas, as well. The students were seven to twelve years old, and the school had six classrooms. She was going to teach all levels. Not all classrooms were occupied. The others were reserved for future use.

We enjoyed a delicious lunch at the Capetta Restaurant and Hotel. It seemed rice dishes were the most popular there, but I asked for simple boiled potatoes with my entree. Happily, my wish was granted.

After lunch, we walked to the end of the road where the hiking part of our outing began. We were so lucky to have two knowledgeable mountain family members, who knew every nook and cranny of the place. It made our trip very special. They got us very close to the mountains. They knew every single curve of the road.

After more enjoyable moments with Werner and Christine, Ruth and I found ourselves flying through a very narrow tunnel on the train, leaving this special place and returning to familiar surroundings once again. Sitting in the train, we began to absorb this special day. It felt good, and we were very thankful as we reflected on our visit. We realized—as we had many times before—how fortunate we were to be in Switzerland, a country of so many unusual treasures. All I can say now is, "Thank you, Werner and Christine, from the bottom of my heart."

My Very Last Flight

ON NOVEMBER 2nd, 2018, my first great-grandson, Liam—short for William—the son of my granddaughter, Rebecca, and her husband, Justin Beere, was born. The bris was scheduled for November 10th.

Ann immediately arranged our flights from San Francisco, California to New York for the event. We decided to spend the night at the Marriott Airport Hotel near SFO before our flight. It was a dark November evening, and with my diminishing eyesight and extremely poor streetlights, I found it most difficult to locate the entrance to the hotel.

The pleasure of waking up to a perfectly clear sky left us with a happy feeling. Leisurely, we had our breakfast, and in no time arrived at the airport. We had requested a wheelchair, a true blessing for people like me. I was ninety-one years old. The volunteers in the airport took special care of us, getting us onto our flight, and the plane landed smoothly in New York. We took a taxi to a hotel near Central Park, close to where Rebecca and her family lived and also, where Justin's parents were staying.

On Sunday, the day of the bris, I held my first great-grandson in my arms for the first time. The feeling was indescribable. The ceremony was led by Rabbi Mollke of their local temple. Addressing the people present—just an intimate circle—Rebecca talked about her Opa and Oma, stating how much we meant to her. I was thankful. It assured me that my husband and I had done something right for the family. With Liam on my lap, I could give him my blessings, knowing full well Opa was right there with us too.

    Ann needed to stay a few extra days in New York, and I knew, with all the special help provided by the airlines, I could fly back home by myself. That night, aboard the aircraft, I clearly realized this was my last flight. I was thankful that I was able to make it to the bris for my oldest great-grandson. I knew that the end of my travels had come, but I had no regrets.

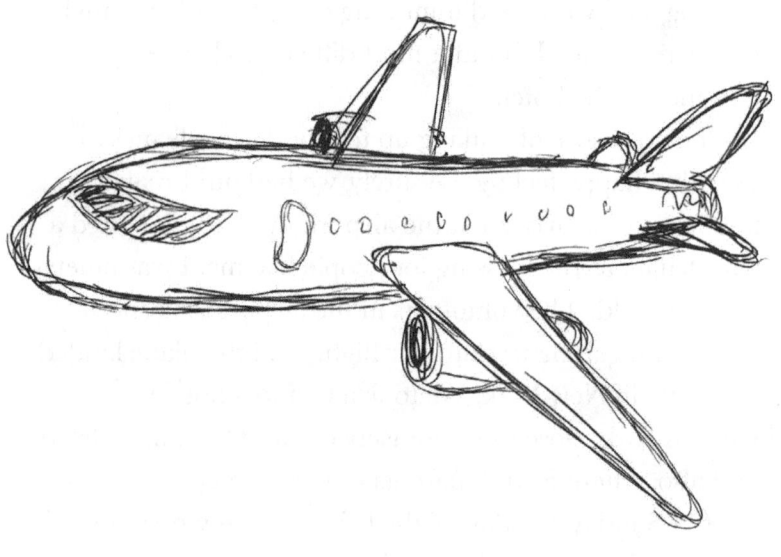

EPILOGUE

THE ORIGIN OF "CARRY ON"

*This story appeared in its original form in **Oma Carries On: Stories from my Life**.*

IN 1939, THE BRITISH MINISTRY of Information under Winston Churchill coined the famous words: "Keep calm and carry on."

Throughout my life with Dr. Bill, I always heard him say, "Carry on" as patients left the office, at the end of phone calls with friends, and at other times too. After he died, patients and friends wrote to me about how much those two words meant to them.

I found information about this phrase on a 2015 calendar, a present from Rebecca.

In 1939, as Britain prepared to enter WW2, the Government turned its attention to the task of bolstering national morale. By the time the war was officially declared, two posters were designed for that specific purpose. They

Elisabeth and Bill ca. 1990

were found on walls and windows across the country.

A third one was created, reserved for a moment of greater need. That poster was only to be used if the Nazi army crossed the British Channel. With white typeface and a crown motif on a solid red background, it read:

KEEP CALM AND CARRY ON

Fortunately, that poster was never needed. More than two million copies were destroyed.

In 2000, Stuart Manley, a bookstore owner in Northern England, discovered a single poster neatly folded at the bottom of a for-used-books drawer. He framed it and hung it in his shop window where it immediately attracted attention from passersby and customers. Manley was able to reproduce the image, and ever since, that poster has sold all over the world.

In 2020–2021, throughout the long year of COVID-19, of sheltering in and mask-wearing and fear of a potentially deadly and easily spread disease, it seemed doubly important to me to have words like these to lift our spirits up. It has been more important than ever to think positively, never to give up, even if we have to be all alone in our apartments for days and days and days.

Yes, we do know, this too shall pass. And so, I say to you, my dear readers, in this *Kaleidoscope* collection, my last ever book: Carry on!

www.ingramcontent.com/pod-product-compliance
Lightning Source LLC
Chambersburg PA
CBHW060418050426
42449CB00009B/2009